Money Magic

Alvin Hall has his own rags-to-riches story. He grew up in Florida, did well at school and was the first person in his family to go to university. After that, he worked as a teacher. He was excited about earning a wage for the first time, and soon found it hard to control his spending. He ran up big bills that he couldn't afford to pay. But Alvin didn't hide from the problem. Instead, he took on an extra job and followed some basic rules. Gradually he got back in control and he hasn't had a serious money problem since!

Alvin now runs a financial services training company. He has presented many popular TV programmes including the award-winning *Your Money or Your Life*, and he appears annually on *The Apprentice – You're Fired*. His books include *Your Money or Your Life* (winner of the 2003 WHSmith People's Choice Best Business Book award) and *Spend Less, Live More*. He lives in New Y

Also by Alvin Hall

Money for Life
Winning with Shares
Your Money or Your Life
You and Your Money
Spend Less, Live More
Plan Now, Retire Happy

Money Magic

Seven simple steps to
true financial freedom

Alvin Hall
With Karl Weber

Hodder & Stoughton Ltd
338 Euston Road
London NW1 3BH

www.hodder.co.uk

HODDER

First published in Great Britain in 2010 by Hodder & Stoughton
An Hachette UK company

1

Copyright © Alvin Hall 2010

A CIP catalogue record for this title is available
from the British Library

ISBN 978 0340 99850 2

Typeset in Stone Serif by Palimpsest Book Production Ltd,
Grangemouth, Stirlingshire

Printed and bound by
Clays Ltd, St Ives plc

Hodder & Stoughton policy is to use papers that are natural,
renewable and recyclable products and made from wood grown in
sustainable forests. The logging and manufacturing processes are
expected to conform to the environmental regulations
of the country of origin.

Money Magic

Dedication

Most of my family never learned the basic facts about money. There were many reasons for this, some personal, others social. But in any case, they never gained the knowledge needed to become free and secure in regard to money.

But most of my family members did have a lot of common sense and a strong desire to make their lives better. And although their lives were often hard, they were not angry or bitter. They often said, 'As long as you are alive and kicking, you can change what will happen in the time to come.' The wisdom of this saying has stayed with me my whole life.

All progress starts with one step forward – or, in this little book about money, with one word, one sentence, or one page. This book is offered to all people who believe that knowledge will help them make their lives better 'in the time to come'. When it does, as my Uncle Son used to say, 'Your soul will look back in wonder.'

Contents

Introduction
My Money Story

As a money expert, I've been on a number of TV programmes to give financial guidance about saving and spending wisely. I've helped people with serious money problems to understand the reasons for their troubles and find answers. I enjoy helping people and I find this work very rewarding.

However, my TV shows have given many people the wrong idea about me. When people meet me, they often say, 'I guess you've always been good with money.'

'Not at all,' I answer. 'In fact, when I was young, I made terrible money choices. I probably made more mistakes than you!' People are always surprised to hear this. Actually, I think some don't even believe me!

I think I know why people find the truth about me surprising. We believe people really remain the same, from childhood to old age. Of course, everyone goes through changes in life. People leave school, get a job, maybe get married or have children. But we usually think that, deep down, we remain the same, no matter how our lives might change on the surface. That's why you hear sayings like, 'You can't teach an old dog new tricks!' The idea is that people's habits never really change.

People often think this way about their money habits. When I chat with people who are having money troubles, they often talk as if they can't ever change. They say things like, 'I've never been good at finances.' 'My parents were bad with money, and so am I.' 'All I know how to do with money is spend it.' 'I wish someone else could take care of my money because I'll never work it out!'

There may be some truth in these statements, but the idea that change is impossible is just wrong. Maybe you've made money mistakes in the past, like many other people. That doesn't mean you must be trapped by those mistakes. Life is about learning and growing. Anyone who is willing to read this book and try the seven steps I suggest can learn to be better with money. I know, because I had to learn the same lessons. I learned them the hard way, by making costly mistakes.

I grew up in a large, hard-working family in a small farming town in Florida, in America. My mother earned money to put food on the table by cleaning other people's homes. This was very hard work, but it didn't pay much, so cash was scarce. Treats like trips to the nearby town were rare. If I fell over when I was playing and tore a hole in my trousers, well, I just had to wear the mended pair until next year, when Mum might have money for a new pair.

When I grew up, I was lucky enough to win a scholarship to a good university. That meant I was able to attend the kind of university my mother could never have paid for. I studied hard and earned good grades. After finishing my course, I went to work as a teacher. It was my first real job, and I was very excited to have it.

Oddly enough, that's when my money troubles began. As a child, I rarely thought about money, and I never missed most of the things I couldn't have. Once I had my wages in my pocket every two weeks, I quickly discovered a world full of great things to buy! I soon learned about the fun of going out to dinner with my friends, going to the theatre and taking holidays. I loved shopping for clothes and pictures, books and music.

I soon got my first credit card.* It seemed like magic. I could buy something I wanted even if I had no money! I just handed over the card, and the shop assistant would give me my nice new item with a smile and a cheerful, 'Come again.'

* See the Word List at the end of this book, where I explain the meaning of money terms like 'credit card'.

When the bill arrived at the end of the month, I didn't have to pay the full amount. I could pay just a few dollars and then go out shopping again. After a while, I reached my credit limit on that card. No problem. I just got a second card, and then a third, and then a fourth.

Before long, I was sinking deeper and deeper into debt. I owed a couple of thousand dollars here, a few hundred there, another thousand somewhere else. It added up to a scary mountain of debt. A time came when I couldn't afford even the minimum payments on my credit cards. I found myself lying awake at night, wondering how I was going to pay my rent.

At last, I said to myself, 'I can't go on this way.' I decided to look honestly at what I'd done wrong. I had to start with the fact that the problem was me, not someone else. The credit card companies weren't to blame. Neither were the shops, with their tempting sales, or my friends, who enjoyed spending money with me, or my boss, who wouldn't pay me enough to cover my bills. The bad choices had been mine, and the only person who could fix the problem was me.

I took a dramatic, painful step. I removed the credit cards from my wallet, grabbed a pair of scissors, and cut the cards into little pieces. (I kept just one card to use when I travelled.) I vowed I would stop spending too much, pay off my bills, and get out of debt. I also vowed I would never fall into the same trap again. In the end, I kept both vows.

Was it easy? No way. It was a struggle, and it will always be a struggle. I still have to fight myself when I see the word 'SALE' in the window of a shop I love. It takes lots of my strength to turn my head away and walk past (and I admit I don't always succeed). But most of the time I keep my money demons – demons like greed, desire and lack of patience – under control.

If you are having money troubles of your own, my story may sound familiar. I'm sure the details are not the same, but the fear and worry are. You're not alone. Millions of people have had the same problems as you and I. At the moment the economy is in trouble. Some people are losing their jobs and struggling to keep up with the bills. Your money problems may be feeling really hard to cope with, but that doesn't mean that you cannot tackle them.

This book has been written to help you master your own money demons. It will teach you how to spot the times and places when you get careless about spending money. It will help you to know your money personality, which is your inner self that guides your money choices –

good and bad. If you are in debt, it will show you how to pay back what you owe and stop being afraid every time the phone rings or a bill arrives in the post. It will teach you how to save, even if your income is barely enough to pay for the things you need. And it will show you how to share your new wisdom about money with the people you love. Your whole family can then enjoy the good things that wise use of money can bring. The results may sound like magic, but the steps it takes to achieve them are simple.

As for me, I now feel I know my own demons and how to control them. A little while ago, I was filming a TV programme in Chester. I passed a fancy shop and saw a stunning watch in the window. I felt as though a button inside me had been pushed, hard! (It was a watch that pushed my button, but for you, it might be something else, like a new car, a sharp new outfit, or a holiday trip you can't afford. But we all have something that pushes our buttons, don't we?)

During a break in filming, I visited the shop. I told myself, 'It's just to look.' As I walked in the door, I felt myself growing weak. The friendly salesman showed me the watch from the window. It was even more handsome up close. Then he said, 'If you like the watch, you may like these, too,' and he showed me a stunning pair of cufflinks. It was easy to picture them shining on my own wrists. Another button had been pushed!

My hand reached for my credit card, but I caught myself just in time. 'I need to think about it,' I said to the salesman, and I walked quickly out of the shop. I knew that the worst thing I could do would be to give in and buy the watch there and then. Taking the time to think about your spending is one simple way to take control of your own bad habits.

Some hours later, I remembered that I already had a pair of cufflinks like those in the shop. 'And I have a couple of watches that tell very good time,' I thought. 'Why buy one more?' My gut desire was fading. The demon had been beaten, at least for today. I felt pleased with myself for being strong, and for not wrecking my monthly budget.

I know that if I can learn to master my money demons, so can you. I also know that, once you do, you'll be more relaxed, happy, and fulfilled than ever before. Money won't control your life any more. Instead, you will be the one in control, using money as a tool to make your life and the lives of the people you love more enjoyable.

Do you like the sound of that? If so, turn the page, and we'll get started.

Step 1.
Track Your Money Habits

The funny thing about money is that most people think about it a lot. They think about wanting it, earning it, and spending it. They fret about the problems caused by the lack of money, and they dream about the things they could do if they had a lot of it. Yet they rarely think about their own money habits, the day-in, day-out actions that shape their financial lives.

This explains how we can get to the end of the week and find ourselves with an empty purse or wallet, yet with no memory of how we spent the money. 'Where does it all go?' we wonder. And then we quickly forget the question, so that the same thing happens next week.

If you want to take charge of your money life, you need to break this habit. You need to become aware of how you relate to money. Once you know where your money comes from and where it goes, you'll be able to make changes to improve your life. You can take control of your spending, and begin to make choices that will give you greater pleasure and peace of mind.

Who knows, you may even get to the end of the week and find a few pounds left in your pocket!

Learning about your money habits isn't hard. In the next few pages, I'll describe eight exercises you can use that will make it easy. You don't have to try them all. Even one or two will help. But the more you try, the better you'll know your own money habits, and the better you'll be able to make useful changes in the ways you relate to money.

1. For one month, write down every time you spend money, as well as the feelings that go with it. Start by buying a little notebook. This will be your money diary. For one month, carry your money diary with you wherever you go. During that time, write down everything you buy, no matter how big or how small. List what you buy and the amount of money you spend. Include things for which you pay cash (like your morning coffee, newspaper or bus fare) and things you buy with a cheque, a credit card, or a debit card (like a new CD or an item of clothing).

At the end of each day, take a moment to write a brief note describing how you feel about that day's spending. Do you feel joy? Guilt? Regret? Sadness? Pleasure? Of course, every day you will write something different. One day you might write, 'I'm so happy about the new shoes I bought today. They'll look great with the outfit I'm wearing tomorrow. I can't wait to see what my friends at work say!' Another day you might write, 'I feel bad about spending so much money on snacks and drinks at the pub tonight. I really meant to save that cash for the weekend. Hope I can do better tomorrow.'

Sometimes keeping the diary will feel like a bore or a nuisance. You'll think about stopping, or skipping a day or two. Don't! The notes you write will tell you a lot about your money habits, good and bad. They will help you see the ways in which money causes you stress and joy. After keeping your money diary for a month, you'll know yourself much better. And as a result, you'll start to be able to make smarter choices about what to do with your money.

2. List your sources of income. Start by thinking about all the people and places you got money from during the past twelve months. As you think, write them down on a piece of paper, along with the amounts you received from each one. A few of these sources will be obvious, like your earnings from your job or any benefits from the government. Others may be easy to forget. Did your spouse, parents or other family members give or lend you money? Did you get money from a boyfriend or girlfriend, or from someone you used to be married to? Did you get paid for doing part-time work? Did you win money from a lottery, a contest, or gambling? Did you get money from a lawsuit or an insurance claim? List all the places you got money from.

Once you've made your list, think about what it tells you about your present and future sources of income. Can you count on the past year's sources of income for next year? Which sources are likely to grow in the future, and which are likely to shrink or go away? Have you been using borrowed money to pay your bills? Have you relied on a one-time source of income that will never come back? What new sources of income can you find?

Thinking hard about these questions can help you figure out whether your future is bright or cloudy, and what you can do to make it better.

3. Study a credit card bill or a bank statement from one year ago. If you have a credit card, or more than one, pull out the bill you paid twelve months ago. If you don't have a credit card, find an old bank statement, which lists the things you spent money on. Look at each item listed. Try to recall what you bought, and think about how much pleasure it gave you. Do you remember the item? Do you remember why you bought it? Do you still have it? If so, do you still use it? Looking back, was it worth buying? Or was it really a waste of money?

Pull out another credit card or bank statement from the past twelve months and repeat this exercise. Count the number of items you bought that had lasting value, and compare this to the number of items you now wish you hadn't bought. What patterns do you see? Are there certain kinds of items you often waste money on? Which kinds of purchases tend to bring you lasting pleasure?

The lessons you learn from this exercise can help you make fewer, smarter purchases in the months to come.

4. Count the number of purchases you made last year. One easy way to do this is to ask your bank or credit card company to send you a list of all your purchases for the year. (Call them and ask for your 'Year-End Summary'.) Count up how many things you bought with your card. Then add your best guess as to the number of things you bought for cash – your daily lunch, bus fares, cups of coffee, and other small items. All together, how many purchases did you make? (The number will probably be in the hundreds.) Is the number much greater than 365 (the number of days in a year)? If so, it means it may be hard for you to go through a day without buying several things. Is there a good reason for this? Is spending money a habit that you control, or does it control you?

5. List your forms of spending that happen without your control. Many people use their bank or credit cards to pay bills and other expenses automatically, without their control. For instance, if you belong to a gym, you may have chosen to pay the monthly fee automatically by direct debit. Some people have many expenses of this kind, including magazine subscriptions, fees for online computer services, gifts to charities, and so on.

Take out your last credit card bill or bank statement, find all the automatic fees, and list them on a separate piece of paper. This form of spending can be a trap. It makes it easy for you to spend money without thinking about it, even on things you no longer use or want. Ask yourself how many of these monthly fees can you reduce or eliminate.

6. List the things you *hate* to spend money on. We all have ways of spending money that we really dislike. Some of these may be needless expenses you can remove by making a change in your life. For example, if you hate paying for your daily commute, maybe you can set your alarm clock for half an hour earlier and start walking or riding a bicycle to work. Not only will you save money, but you'll be fitter as well.

If you dislike having to pay for simple repairs to your car or your house, think about learning how to make some of those repairs yourself. Many people find it fun to learn how to change their own spark plugs or mend a leaking tap, and it's a good way of saving money as well.

Eating out at a nice restaurant with your friends can be costly, and sometimes people find themselves spending too much because they feel they have to keep up with their friends (who may earn more than they do). What about asking your friends to visit you next weekend, with everyone bringing a home-made dish to share? You and your friends may find that this way of sharing a meal is even more fun than eating out.

7. List your five best and five worst purchases. Think back to all the ways you spent money last year. Make a list of the five things you did with money that improved your life the most. Then make a list of your five worst money mistakes, choices that made your life a little worse or that were a waste. What were the reasons behind each of these choices, good or bad? What can you learn from them that will help you make better choices next year?

There's no single right or wrong way to make these lists. One person's clever choice may be another person's mistake. For Molly, spending £600 on a week's holiday at a fancy beach resort may have helped her clear her head after a tough year at work. Maybe it gave her the boost she needed to start looking for a better job on her return home. For Cynthia, the same holiday may have pushed her to the limit on her credit card. Going deep into debt may have eventually spoiled any pleasure she might have taken from her days in the sun.

Only you can define your best and worst uses of money. Just be honest about it, and use your two lists as a guide to making better choices in the future.

8. Test your money will-power. You can also learn more about your money habits by trying to change them. Right now, I am testing my own will-power in a way that is simple but that

I find very hard. For one year, I am not going to buy a shirt. (I already have forty shirts of all kinds, and I love to get new ones.)

In the past, I've tested myself in other ways. For example, I once locked away my credit cards for a month and forced myself to pay for things only in cash. This test made me more aware of my spending and forced me to think hard about what I really needed.

Small tests like this can help you become more self-confident. When you pass the test, you'll feel proud of your power to control yourself and make wiser choices every day. And even if you fail the test, you will learn some useful things about yourself. Which money habits have the greatest hold over you? Which money habits are easy to change? Which ones really hurt? Being able to answer these questions will make you a better money manager in the long run.

Most people have only a vague sense of how they relate to money. They rarely think about how they get money, how they use it, and the effect it has on their lives. The goal of all eight exercises is the same: to help you know more about the role of money in your life. How does money bring you pleasure? How does it cause you regret, worry, or sadness? Which of your money habits would you like to change? Which ones would you like to strengthen?

Answering these questions is a good first step towards improving your relationship with money.

Step 2.
Learn About Your Money Style

Being good with money isn't just about numbers: the amount you earn, the amount you spend, and the amount you save. If it were, then everyone could learn to be good with money by learning maths at school. But we've all heard about people with lots of education who waste millions and end up poor, while other people who never learned maths are good at saving and end up rich.

Handling money wisely isn't only about knowing the numbers. It's also about knowing yourself, what makes you act the way you do. And it's about knowing how to *change* the ways you act so that you enjoy greater power over money and more freedom in your life. In other words, it's about your money style – knowing it, and making it work for you.

Some people seem to find it easy to know themselves and to control the ways they act. Other people struggle. They find it hard to explain why they act as they do. They say things like, 'I don't know why I can't stop spending.

The money just seems to vanish!' Or, 'No matter how hard I try, I just can't save money. I guess I don't have what it takes, whatever that is!'

I understand how a person's money style can cause trouble. I come from a big family. I have six brothers and sisters, and lots of other relatives. I also have many friends who are rich, poor, and in-between. And as a money expert, I've talked to thousands of people about their money styles. I've met people with almost every money style you can think of, good, bad, smart, silly, brilliant, and just plain crazy!

One member of my family stands out in my mind, and in my fears. I'll call her Jane (not her real name). No matter how much money Jane gets, she always spends it all, and more! She always ends up with big money trouble, owing money to lots of people, who call her day and night to ask for payment. Why does this happen? Because Jane never takes the time to think about her money style and to try to change it. All of us who know Jane and care about her wonder, 'What will it take for Jane to get her life in order?' We worry that it will never happen, that Jane will go to her grave without ever knowing the happiness that comes from learning how to *enjoy* using money wisely.

Whether you have lots of money or only a

little, it's very important to know your money style. In the next few pages, I'll help you figure out what your money style may be. You may see things that remind you of yourself. Or you may see things that reflect the money style of someone close to you – a husband, wife, parent, sister, brother, child, or friend. But the most important goal is to learn about yourself, so that you can begin to make smarter money choices. So as you read, ask yourself the question, 'Does this remind me of myself?'

The Big Spender

One very common money style is that of the Big Spender (also known as the 'shopaholic'). If you are a Big Spender, shopping is a huge part of your life. You think about shopping a lot, and you visit shops every time you have a free hour or two. Spending money excites you. You get a small thrill when you take out your credit card or reach into your pocket or purse for a handful of notes. And you feel very happy when you carry home a bag filled with new items. Shopping is your life!

The Big Spender says things like, 'I just *had* to have it!' 'It was such a bargain, I couldn't say no.' And, 'After all, I deserve a little fun!'

Most Big Spenders have two big problems. First, they think that what they *want* and what they *need* are the same thing. A Big Spender may own ten pairs of shoes, but still think they *need* the nice new pair they spotted on their lunch break. Or a Big Spender may have a car that works just fine, but still think they *need* to trade it in for a newer car that's more stylish and sexy-looking. Importantly, a want is not the same as a need!

Second, Big Spenders use shopping as a way to cure some inner hurt. The thrill of spending money helps them forget about a problem they don't want to face. This might be loneliness, sadness, anger, guilt, shame, or worry. The problem, of course, is that spending too much does nothing to solve the real trouble. All it does is add another source of pain: debts that the Big Spender will struggle to repay.

What to Do?

What should you do if you are a Big Spender? First, keep yourself and your money out of harm's way. Stop visiting the shopping centre or the online shopping sites every day. Go to the shops just once a week, and make a list of what you can afford to buy beforehand. This change in habit can make it easier for you to change your spending ways. Here are some other ideas that can help the Big Spender get his or her life under control.

- **Find a new way to spend your time**. There are lots of ways to have fun without spending money. Take up a new hobby or sport, join a club, or start working out. Or you may want to try doing volunteer work. You could help your elderly neighbours, tutor some children, or work at a local hospital.

- **Use cash instead of a bank or credit card**. (Leave your card at home so you won't be tempted to break this rule.) As you see the stack of notes getting thinner in your wallet or purse, you will *have* to spend less.

- **Don't let yourself buy on impulse**. When you see something you want to buy, hold back. Tell yourself, 'I'll think about it first.' Then take a walk, go for a jog, or watch a little television. An hour or two later, you may find the desire to buy has gone away.

If you are a Big Spender, try these ideas. At first, you'll find them hard. You may have one good day of success followed by one bad day of failure and over-spending. That's all right. What matters is to keep trying, and to slowly get control of the bad money habits that are making your life so painful.

The Cheapskate

If you are a Cheapskate, spending money is hard for you. Even letting a 5p coin out of your grasp seems to hurt. You can't understand why other people enjoy spending, because the only pleasure you get from money comes from saving it. You may be the envy of your friends because you have a lot of money in the bank. But you never enjoy some of the simple things other people like, such as a meal in a restaurant, a holiday in the sun, or a stylish new outfit, because you can't bear to part with any of your money.

The Cheapskate often says things like, 'I'm not going to buy that because I bet I can get it much cheaper.' 'Oh, that's too much. I can remember when the same thing cost half the price.' And, 'No, I won't be joining you. Money is tight right now.' (In truth, it isn't the money that is tight!)

Being a Cheapskate isn't all bad. If you are a Cheapskate, you will never over-spend or lose everything to debt. But you will miss out on many of the good things in life. A Cheapskate shivers all winter because they won't turn up the heat in their house or flat. They skip outings with their friends and go for years without a new suit of clothes or a new car, even when the old ones are falling apart. What's worse, a Cheapskate's family may suffer. I've known Cheapskates who refused to support their children through university, even with thousands of pounds sitting idle in the family bank account.

What to Do?

If you love someone who is a Cheapskate, you need to accept his or her money style. Don't expect the Cheapskate to become like you. Instead, find ways to enjoy being with your Cheapskate friend or relative. If he or she won't go out to dinner, stay home and cook a nice meal together instead. And accept the idea that you will have to find ways to pay for your own choices rather than counting on money from the pocket of a Cheapskate.

And what if you suspect that you may be a Cheapskate? Use these ideas to improve your money style.

- **Try doing new things** that are within your comfort range. If you can't force yourself to eat at a nice restaurant, try going with friends or family to a simple place where the meals are cheaper. If you can't handle a holiday at a swanky resort, enjoy the fun of planning a bargain trip by bus or car, saving money as you see the sights.

- **Learn to accept good things from others**. Many Cheapskates feel upset when friends or family members give them gifts. Practise changing this habit, and try to enjoy giving gifts to others in return. Slowly, you may find yourself discovering that spending money (in small amounts) can really be fun.

- **Make a plan for spending money**. For example, have your family been begging you to get some new clothes and to stop wearing the same outfits you've had for the last twenty years? If so, plan a shopping trip. 'I'll go to the shopping centre and pick two nice outfits, no more! One for winter and one for summer.' Making a plan can help a Cheapskate feel in control.

The Ostrich

You may have seen pictures of this long-necked bird with its head buried in the sand. The bird thinks it can avoid danger by not looking at the thing that it's frightened of. Sadly, it doesn't work, and it doesn't work for people with the money style of the Ostrich, either.

The Ostrich tries to avoid money problems by hiding from them. He or she ignores basic facts about money. Ask an Ostrich how much money they make, what they spend on different things, how much they save or how much money they will need to retire, and their answer will always be the same. 'I don't know.'

If you are an Ostrich, you may not open any post that looks as if it relates to your money. Bank statements, credit card bills, notices of cheques that have bounced, all go straight from the post into a drawer or the rubbish bin. When money news or advice pops up on the radio or the telly, the Ostrich quickly changes the channel. The motto of the Ostrich is, 'Out of sight, out of mind.'

The Ostrich talks a lot about how much they hate having to deal with money. They say things like, 'Money is so complicated, it's all too much for me.' 'I just don't have the time to fuss with my finances.' Or, 'I work so hard at my job, why should I have to put in more work hours coping with something as boring and silly as money?'

Sometimes, the Ostrich talks as if money is just 'too crude' or 'too vulgar' to think about, as if ignoring money makes them better than other people.

The truth, of course, is that the Ostrich is *afraid* of money. The Ostrich worries that they can't understand money questions; they're worried about feeling stupid or doing something foolish that will cost them a lot of money. They may also feel overwhelmed, as if their money problems are a giant flood of troubles that will sweep them away to their doom. Like a helpless animal, they bury their head, hoping to ignore the pain they know is coming.

What to Do?

If you're an Ostrich, you need to learn to manage the money fears that control you. You need to realise that any money problems you face can be dealt with, as long as you tackle them one step at a time. Here are some ideas that will help.

- **Every day, handle one bill or statement**. If money problems have been building up, spend a few minutes each day working on just one problem. Sit down, open up your drawer, take out one bill or statement, and don't get up until the problem has been dealt with. This might mean paying a bill, checking to make sure the balance of your current account is correct and up-to-date, making a phone call to ask for more time to pay, or moving money from one account to another. But no matter what it takes, don't get up until you solve one problem. Then forget about your money worries until the same time tomorrow.

- **Work on money problems at the time of day when you are at your best**. I am a morning person. When I get up, my mind is clear, and I feel ready to get things done. I also find that the weekend is the perfect time for me to deal with money matters because then I get fewer phone calls to distract me. For you, the right time may be different, perhaps Monday evening or Wednesday afternoon. Choose your best time and use it to start a good money habit.

- **Plan a simple money routine**. Schedule regular money tasks for certain days of the month. You might pay your rent on the 1st,

28

pay your other bills on the 5th, review your chequebook on the 10th, put money into savings on the 12th, and so on. Using a routine that divides your money tasks into small, easy steps will prevent money problems from growing into a huge, scary mountain.

The Cynic

The Cynic sees all money matters as part of a big game in which banks and other groups are trying to trick, cheat, and rob the rest of us. If you are a Cynic, your goal in life is to play the game even better than the banks or the government. You use clever dodges and schemes to enrich yourself and prevent 'them' from scamming you.

The Cynic is proud of 'knowing the score', of understanding how the money world *really* works, better than other people. For the Cynic, taxes are a rip-off, saving is for suckers, and the stock market is a casino in which all the bets are rigged. Even working for a living is something only losers waste their time on. Cynics often start businesses that they think will make a lot of money with little effort. When these projects fail, they become bitter, blaming others who don't want 'the little people' to succeed.

The Cynic spends a lot of time talking about

the secrets that the people in charge of money don't want us to know. 'The smart move is to buy property with no deposit!' 'Futures and options, that's how the bankers get rich. All I need is a hot tip from someone in the know!' Or, 'Getting other people to provide the money and take the risk – that's the key to making it big!'

Sometimes, people become Cynics starting with a few tricks that seem simple and harmless. For instance, they may move their debt to a new credit card that charges little or no interest for a set period of time. Then, when higher interest rates kick in, they move to a different card, and then to another, and another. The problem is that, over time, people using this trick end up owning more and more credit cards. And the more cards they own, the greater their chance of debt. In the end, the whole thing comes crashing down, and buries the Cynic.

What to Do?

If you are a Cynic, or are tempted to become one, try these ideas to gain a more sound, sensible approach to money matters.

- **KISS: Keep it simple, stupid!** Sometimes the best ways to improve your money life are the simplest ones. Spend a little less than you earn. Look for ways to save money on basic things like rent, your mortgage, the car you drive, the food you eat, the clothes you wear. Avoid going into debt. Put your extra money in the bank. More people have solved their money problems through simple steps like these than through fancy tricks, schemes, or 'hot tips' peddled by 'insiders'.

- **Teach yourself about how the money world works**. Go to any bookshop or library and ask about classic money books, like *The Millionaire Next Door* or any book by Warren Buffett or Peter Lynch. You'll soon learn that the richest people in the world got that way by being careful with their money and putting it into safe, simple saving and investment plans that grew over time.

- **Devote your time and effort to work and achievement**. Instead of working on complex schemes to get around the rules on taxes or paying your debts, spend the same amount of effort on your career. Work hard, learn new skills, and look for jobs at companies that are well run and growing quickly. As your career grows, so will your income. Soon you'll find yourself at the top of the money heap, without having to trick anybody.

The Balanced Style

Do you have one of the money styles I've described? Are you a Big Spender, a Cheapskate, an Ostrich, or a Cynic? Maybe you have a style that combines two or more of the styles. That's not unusual. Everyone has a money style that is unique and that helps to define the problems they will face in handling money.

Your goal should be to create a money style that is *balanced*. This means being able to manage your money in a way that avoids the problems caused by going too far in any direction. You should be able to enjoy shopping without over-spending; to save without becoming stingy; to deal with money matters without becoming too fearful; and to make good money plans without becoming cynical. Being aware of your money style and the strengths and weaknesses that go with it is the first step to reaching balance.

The second step is developing money habits that help you improve your style. If your biggest problem is spending too much, try the ideas I've offered to get your shopping habit under control. If you hide from money problems the way an ostrich hides from its enemies, use the tricks I've described to tackle those problems one easy step at a time.

No one is perfect. You won't make wise money choices every time. But every time you remember to do the right thing, you will make your good money habits stronger. Over the coming weeks, months, and years, you will become better and better at choosing the best money path. At the same time, practice will make it easier and easier for you to do so.

Everyone must create a unique money style with a balance of its own. Some people need to earn a lot of money to be happy, while others are content with much less. Some people need to own two houses, while others prefer a small house with a pretty garden, or are happy to rent a comfortable flat in their favourite city. Some people must go on holiday to five-star hotels, while others like nothing better than hiking in the woods and sleeping under the stars. Everyone can enjoy a balanced money style, as long as the choices they make are the right ones *for them*.

Now that you've learned something about your own money style, along with its strengths and weaknesses, let's take a look at some of the steps you can take to improve your money balance and achieve greater financial freedom. For many people, that begins with solving the problem of debt.

Step 3.
Get Out of Debt

Being deep in debt is like being in water above your head. And if you've ever faced this problem, you know it is much easier to get into debt than it is to get out. But the most important thing is that you *can* get out. There are ways to escape the deep waters of debt and return safely to dry land, where you can live a normal life again. So don't give up hope, even if your debts have become very large. In the next few pages, you'll learn how to get past your debt problems and start building a better financial future for yourself and your family.

As you may know, more people are in debt today than ever before. The current financial crisis has shown that many of us have borrowed far more than we can afford, and now we are struggling. Many people think this means that the problem is not the fault of those who borrowed the money. Instead, they want to blame the credit card companies that let them borrow. 'The credit card companies are greedy,' they say. 'They're also dishonest. They offer credit cards to people who really can't afford them, and who may not know how to handle debt. And some of the risks in credit card debt are hidden in the small print of the credit card agreements. No wonder so many people get into trouble. After all, they don't even know what they agree to when they accept a credit card deal.'

There is some truth in these words. Credit card companies *are* greedy. But that is no surprise. They are in business to make money, and the more they make, the happier they are. It's also true that in recent years, credit cards have been given to some people who shouldn't have them. People have been urged to go into debt to buy things they don't really need. The mountains of debt we now have to deal with are the result.

But for most people who are in trouble because of debt, the real danger is not in the credit card. It's in themselves. The card is just a piece of plastic. It can't harm you if you control its use, and that means being in control of yourself.

The Six Most Common Feelings that Drive People into Debt

The real trouble comes from six deadly emotions – those feelings that lead people to misuse credit. Money problems aren't mainly about money. More often, they're about how you *think* about money. Even before you get out of debt, you need to look at how your thoughts and feelings got you into debt in the first place. If you don't change your thinking, you may find yourself back in debt again very quickly. (I know because I've seen it happen many times!)

So if you are over your head in debt, ask yourself which of these six emotions you have been feeling.

1. **Denial ('Money problems? Who, me?!')** Denial means refusing to face facts, acting as if all is well when deep inside you know that trouble is growing. Denial lets you ignore your money troubles by saying to yourself and others, 'Oh, I don't have a problem. I just need to pay off a few bills. The money will come in any day now!' If you remain in a state of denial, you may soon find yourself beyond help.

Think about these questions. Are you keeping money secrets from the people closest to you, such as your husband or your wife? Do you respond with lies or even anger when well-meaning friends or family members offer you help with your money problems? Do you spend money you can't afford in an effort to hide the money problems you face? These are signs of denial that can quickly make your money troubles much worse.

2. **Entitlement ('I deserve it!')** If you find yourself saying, 'I deserve it' when you buy something, especially when you buy something you can't afford, it's a bad sign that you are spending for foolish reasons.

The feeling of entitlement can have many sources. Some people feel that spending money will impress their friends, neighbours, or relatives. Others choose to believe 'they deserve it' because they want to feel they are smarter, better, or 'cooler' than others. Still others feel they deserve costly things because they work hard or because their family members don't appreciate them.

Whatever the reason, a sense of entitlement almost always leads to trouble. In the real world, people can't buy things just because they 'deserve' them. Instead, they need to buy things when they can *afford* them. There's a big difference!

3. **Compensation ('Now it's *my* turn!')** Compensation is about making up for the pains of the past. Many grown-up people are still living with memories of the things they couldn't have

when they were children. Thinking about the toys, clothing, and other things they couldn't have while growing up, or maybe about the love from Mum and Dad that was never enough, they still feel a sense of loss.

Those strong feelings have a way of coming to the surface when we become adults and get our first credit card. Now all the goodies we dreamed about as children can be ours just by handing over that little plastic card. (Of course, most of us buy 'grown-up toys' like cars, clothing, furniture, and appliances rather than dolls or sandpits, but the idea is the same.)

The problem is that this feeling from the past may become an excuse for over-spending in the present. As the debts and interest charges grow every month, the hurts from your past may begin to damage your future.

4. **Crowd-Think ('Everyone's doing it, so why shouldn't I?')** Crowd-think is the feeling that a problem you have in common with many other people can't be very serious. When you find yourself thinking, 'Everyone's doing it, so why shouldn't I?' you are giving in to crowd-think.

Of course, crowd-think can lead to big trouble. If many of your friends have problems with drugs or drinking, crowd-think may lead you to have the same difficulties. And over-spending through credit may come about in the same way. You watch your friends pull out their plastic at the local shopping centre or pub, and it's easy to follow their lead.

But in the end, of course, there is a price to be paid. The supposedly 'free' money that the credit card provides is far from free. Add in the interest charges and fees, and the things you buy on credit could end up costing far more than if you'd paid in cash to begin with.

5. **Empty Hope ('Something will turn up soon!')** Maybe you've been the victim of empty hope, the feeling that somehow your debt problems will solve themselves. Empty hope can take several forms. Some people like to think that a great job with a big pay rise is just around the corner. Others believe their parents will bail them out, either with a handsome gift of money or (more sadly) with a large sum they will inherit when their parents die. And still others dream that the man or woman of their dreams will come along and solve the problem. The idea here is that Prince Charming, or Princess Charming, will be not only beautiful, kind, and sexy, but also very rich! In reality, of course, these rosy dreams rarely come true. If you are

sinking into debt because of empty hope, you need to break free from this emotion. Don't pretend that you are simply being 'positive' or 'optimistic' about the future, while others are 'negative' or 'gloomy'. Face facts. You are fooling yourself, and in the long run that can only bring you trouble.

6. **Fear ('I can't bear to face another bill!')** The sight of rows of numbers, especially if they have pound signs attached, makes some people react like rabbits frozen in the headlights of a car. If you suffer from this problem, don't let your fear of numbers become an excuse to sink into debt. The truth is that you probably have a pretty good idea about what you need to do to solve your money woes. Spend less, earn more, pay your debts, and save money. And if you need more advice, there are plenty of ways to learn, including this book.

The real first step towards handling your money more wisely is understanding how your emotions are hurting you. Stop blaming someone or something else. Instead, take control of your feelings and let them know who's boss.

How Bad Is Your Debt Problem?

To start the process of getting out of debt, you need a clear picture of your money situation. Forming such a picture involves a few simple steps, which I'll explain below.

Make a Debt Worksheet

On a piece of paper, write a list of all the debts you owe. You'll create a table with four columns, from left to right. (See the example opposite). This is your *debt worksheet*. For each debt, write the following:

- Column 1. The name of the lender (which may be a credit card company, a bank, a shop, or a person who has lent you money). For this exercise, you *don't* need to include your home mortgage. But if you have a second mortgage, or if you owe money on a home equity loan, *do* include this debt here.

- Column 2. The current balance (that is, the total amount of money you owe, *not* one month's payment).

- Column 3. The annual percentage interest rate (APR) charged (that is, the amount of interest the lender charges you for the money you've borrowed).

- Column 4. The minimum payment required (that is, the smallest amount you *must* pay every month).

Example of a Debt Worksheet

Column 1	Column 2	Column 3	Column 4
Lender	Balance	APR	Minimum Repayment
Company A	£2000	22%	£110
Company B	£1500	19%	£70
Company C	£800	17%	£40
Company D	£400	12%	£28
TOTAL	£4700		£248

You may find it hard to work out the APR you are paying on each debt or loan. Look closely at your monthly bill. The APR may be listed somewhere in the small print. If not, find the paperwork the lender gave you when you first opened the account or accepted the loan. It lists the conditions of your loan. The APR should appear somewhere on one of the pages. If you can't find it, call your lender and ask for the APR. Once you get the number, list it on your piece of paper in

Column 3. As you'll see later, this is an important piece of information.

Now, add up the current balances for all your loans, and write the sum at the bottom of Column 2. (You may want to use a calculator to help with this step.) Also add up the minimum payments you must make each month, and write this sum at the bottom of Column 4.

Create a Simple Budget Worksheet

Next, you need to figure out how your debts compare to your total money situation. To do this, you need to create a simple budget, which shows where your money is coming from and where it is going. Get out another piece of paper, on which you'll create your *budget worksheet.* (see the example opposite). List the following for the past month:

- Column 1. All your sources of income (for example, your wages, any benefits, loans from friends or family) and the amount you received from each one.

- Column 2. All your fixed, unchanging expenses (for example, your mortgage or rent, council taxes, gas and electricity bills,

Example of a Budget Worksheet

Column 1		Column 2		Column 3	
Income		**Fixed Expenses**		**Other Expenses**	
Take-home pay:	£1500	Mortgage/rent:	£500	Dinners out:	£60
Part-time work:	£150	Gas and electricity:	£150	Entertainment:	£150
Benefits/ loans/gifts:	£100	Taxes:	£100	Clothing:	£70
		Travel:	£80	Gifts:	£50
		Food at home:	£250	Other:	£70
		Debt repayment:	£248		
		Other:	£100		
Total income:	£1750	Total fixed:	£1428	Total other:	£400

telephone, food, travel costs) and the amount you spent on each. Include all the expenses from the month, even if you used a credit card and paid only part of the cost at the end of the month.

- Column 3. All your other expenses, things you spent money on when you didn't have to (for example, dinners out, holidays, clothing, gifts, entertainment) and the amount you spent on each. Again, include all expenses, even if you used a credit card and didn't pay the full amount at the end of the month.

Now add up all your income, and put the sum at the bottom of Column 1. Add up your fixed expenses, and put the sum at the bottom of Column 2. Then add up your other expenses, and put the sum at the bottom of Column 3. Finally, add the sum of Column 2 and the sum of Column 3, to figure out your *total* expenses. Write this sum at the very bottom of the budget worksheet.

All by themselves, these numbers can tell you a lot. Look closely at your budget worksheet, and think about the following questions.

- Which is greater: your total income (Column

1) or your total expenses (bottom of the page)? If your income is greater, you have a chance to save. If your expenses are greater, you are going further into debt and that means trouble ahead.

- Which is greater: your fixed expenses (Column 2) or your other expenses (Column 3)? For most people, if your other expenses are greater, you may be spending too much on non-urgent things. Look for ways to save.

- How much do you expect your income (Column 1) to change from month to month? If your income varies by more than a small amount, you could be in trouble. Again, look for ways to save, so that you won't suffer much if your income falls.

- Did you have any emergencies or major expenses during this month? For example, did you have to fix your car or an appliance? Did you have to pay any vet bills this month? If *not*, you may face trouble in the future. Most people have emergencies or special costs from time to time. If your total income is spent every month, this may cause you serious problems.

Figure Out Your Debt Burden

You've figured out how much you owe to various lenders, and you've also created a simple budget that shows where your money comes from and goes every month. Now it's time to put the two together and work out how much debt is a problem for you. To do this, get the debt worksheet and the budget worksheet that you have already created, and use them to answer the following questions. (Again, a calculator will be helpful.)

- What percentage of your total income is your total debt? To figure this out, take your total debt balance (Column 1 on your debt worksheet) and divide it by your total monthly income (Column 1 on your budget worksheet) and then multiply the answer by 100.

  If the sum is 200 or more (that is 200 per cent of your total income), then debt is a real problem for you. You need to work on bringing your debt down as quickly as possible. For example, if your total debt balance is £4700, as in the debt worksheet on page 43, and your monthly income is £1750, as shown on the budget worksheet on page 45, you would work out the percentage this way:

$$£4700 \div £1750 \quad = 2.69$$
$$2.69 \times 100 \quad = 269 \text{ (269 per cent)}.$$

This is a high percentage. You need to get to work right away on reducing the amount of debt you have.

• What percentage of your total income is the minimum payment on your debt? To work this out, take your total minimum payments required (Column 4 on your debt worksheet) and divide it by your total monthly income (Column 1 on your budget worksheet) and then multiply by 100.

If the result is more than 15 (15 per cent of your total income), then you are definitely in trouble. You may have found that you are having problems reducing the amount you owe, since your monthly payments are covering only the interest charged by the lenders, not the original amount of money you borrowed. For example, if your total minimum payment required is £248, as shown on the debt worksheet on page 43, and your total monthly income is £1750, as shown on the budget worksheet on page 45, the percentage is:

$$£248 \div £1750 = 0.14$$
$$0.14 \times 100 = 14 \text{ (14 per cent)}$$

This is just below the 15 per cent danger amount – too close for comfort really.

These questions are designed to help you figure out whether or not debt is a very big problem for you. For many people, it is. If you find the results troubling, read on. I'll explain below how to start working your way out of debt.

If the amount you owe and your monthly minimum payment fall below the guidelines I've offered, that's good. But it doesn't mean you shouldn't think about getting out of debt. For most people, the road to long-term financial success begins with becoming debt-free. When you owe nothing, you save all the money that you previously had to spend on interest. This creates the chance to build up savings every month. And the savings you build will, over time, give you the chance to enjoy such great things as a dream home, a fine education for your children and, in the long-term, a secure retirement.

So no matter whether your debt burden is big or small, I hope you'll start getting out of debt. The sooner you become debt-free, the greater your chance of reaching true financial happiness.

Create Your Get-Out-of-Debt Action Plan

When you have money problems, it's easy to dream about someone or something coming into your life to make everything better. It could be winning the lottery, falling in love with someone who is rich, or getting a huge gift of money from a relative or some stranger. But while you are dreaming, the debt is still there, growing. So instead of trying to dream your debts away, you should create an action plan to reduce them. It's not as hard as you may think. Just follow the steps below.

Reduce Your Interest Costs

Interest is the cost of borrowing money. When you take out a loan or buy something on credit, the lender charges you interest every month until the debt is repaid. The longer you take to pay back the money, the more interest you must pay. If you buy something with a credit card and make only the minimum payment required each month, it will take you years to pay off the debt. And by the time the debt is gone, you will most likely have paid several times the purchase price in interest!

As you can see, interest on debt is deadly. So the first thing you should do to control your debt burden is to reduce the amount of interest you have to pay.

Here is where the annual percentage rate (APR) on each of your debts comes in. Find the APR for your various debts in Column 3 of your debt worksheet. Which debts have the highest APR? Which debt has the lowest? Your first goal should be to move as much of your debt as possible from high-APR lenders to a low-APR lender. This will save you money every month on interest charges.

There are two ways to do this. One is to move some or all of your debt to a loan or credit card with the lowest annual APR you can find. Suppose you owe money to two credit card companies. Let's say that Company A has an APR of 20 per cent, while Company B has an APR of 12 per cent. If you have enough available credit from Company B, you should use it to pay off the debt you owe to Company A (or as much as you can). You will still have to pay the debt, but the interest rate cost will be lower. That will save you money over time.

Another way to reduce the APR you pay is by asking your bank to give you a special kind of loan called a *consolidation loan*. With this kind of loan, the bank lends you enough money to pay off all your other debts. Then, each month, you just have to pay one bill to the bank until the total amount you borrowed is repaid. If you can get a consolidation loan with a lower APR than the debts you now have, you can save a lot of money on interest.

But be careful about signing up for a consolidation loan. There are lots of adverts for such loans on TV. Some make the loans sound like a magic wand that makes debt vanish. Others make the lenders sound like kind-hearted souls whose only wish is to help you get out of debt. In fact, like all lenders, they plan to make a profit from lending to you. There's nothing wrong with that, but it means you must study their promises or claims with care.

If you ask your bank about a consolidation loan, be sure to find out what the APR on the loan will be. Take out a consolidation loan only if the APR is lower than what you are now paying.

Also, you will have a choice of how long to take to repay the money. This is called the *term* of the loan. The term could be one year, two years, three years, five years, or some other length. The banker will explain how much you must repay each month based on the term of the loan. The longer the term, the smaller your monthly bill.

But since you are paying bills to the bank for a longer time, the total amount you must repay will be greater when the term of the loan is longer.

My advice is to choose the *shortest* term you can afford. It will be a little harder to repay a larger amount each month. But your debt will go away faster, and the total amount of interest you must pay will be much less. You could save thousands of pounds in interest by paying off your debt more quickly! Please do this if you can.

Pay off Your Worst Debts First

You may not be able to move all of your debt to a single credit card or a single loan. Instead, you may find that you still have a list of several debts to repay. If so, the next step in reducing your debt is to make a repayment plan. The best idea is to pay off the worst debts first – that is, those with the highest APR. Here's how to do that.

Make up a new debt worksheet. On this worksheet, list your debts in order based on the size of the APR. The debt you list first should be the one with the highest APR. Then list the debt with the second-highest APR, and so on, until all your debts are listed.

Next, look at your budget worksheet. This

gives you a simple picture of your monthly income and expenses. Using this, decide the amount of money you can afford to spend each month on repaying debts. Make the amount as large as you can. (Yes, this may mean cutting the amount you spend on other things.)

Once you've picked an amount to repay each month, you must decide how much to use for each debt. To do this, start by listing the minimum amount you *must* repay for each debt. (You listed this in Column 4 of your original debt worksheet.) Add up these amounts. Subtract the sum from the total amount you plan to use for repayments. The result should be used as an extra repayment for the debt at the top of your list, the debt with the highest APR. That is your 'worst' debt, so it's the debt you want to repay first.

Here's an example. Suppose you have four debts, with the balances, APRs, and minimum repayments shown below.

Lender	Balance	APR	Minimum Repayment
Company A	£2300	22%	£110
Company B	£2200	19%	£95
Company C	£1950	17%	£80
Company D	£1045	12%	£52

Let's suppose you decide that you can spend £400 each month to repay your debts. Add up the minimum repayment amounts for the four loans. (Use a calculator if you like.)

$$£110 + £95 + £80 + £52 = £337$$

This is less than £400, so you will use the difference, the 'extra' money, to pay off your worst debt, which is the debt you owe to Company A.

$$£400 - £337 = £63$$

So you have an extra £63 to pay to Company A on top of the minimum payment.

$$£110 + £63 = £173$$

So you will make a payment of £173 to Company A when you start your new repayment plan. You'll also make the minimum payments to Companies B, C, and D.

You see how this works. By sending the largest amount to Company A each month, you will be paying off your worst debt first. In a few months, you will have totally paid off Company A. Then your debt to Company B will become your worst debt, and you will start sending it the largest amount you can. By using this plan, you will reduce your worst debts first. The plan will save you lots of money, thousands of pounds in the long run, if your debt burden is great.

If Your Debt Is too Great, Talk with Your Lenders

For most people, the steps I've just explained will be a good way of getting out of debt. But for some people, stronger steps are needed. This may be the case if your debt is so great that you can't afford to make even the minimum payments each month. You may find that you owe so much money that you can't keep up with the debt while also taking care of the normal costs of life – such as rent, food, the phone bill, and so on.

If you face this problem, it's time to talk with your lenders. Pick up the phone and call the number on your bill. Explain that you are having trouble paying off your debts and that you'd like to discuss what can be done. There are two things you can ask for.

1. **Ask your lenders to** *freeze* **your interest charges**. If they agree to do this, it means they will, for a time, stop charging interest on the amount of money you owe. You will still have to make monthly payments, but

the payments you make will be clearing more of the actual debt. A lender may be willing to do this if you have a short-term money problem; for instance, if you lose your job or have a large expense to deal with, like a car crash.

2. **Ask your lenders to lower your minimum monthly payment.** If they agree to do this, it will take you longer to pay off the balance you owe. But it can help you get through a hard time while still handling the daily costs of life.

Most lenders are willing to help people who have debt problems and are sincere about fixing them. If you've been making your payments on time and are honest about your situation, they will probably want to help you get back on your feet. After all, it is better for them to get smaller payments each month than nothing at all.

On the other hand, if you've been missing payments, ignoring phone calls from your lenders, or failing to make payments that you've promised, your lenders may not be willing to talk. So play fair with the people you owe money to. It will help you in the long run.

If you find yourself in a debt situation that is

so bad you just don't know what to do, you may need to go further for help. Here are three groups you may want to call.

Citizen's Advice
Phone: Find your local branch in the phone book
Website: www.citizensadvice.org.uk

Consumer Credit Counselling Service
Phone: 0800 138 1111
Website: www.cccs.co.uk

National Debt Line
Phone: 0808 808 4000
Website: www.nationaldebtline.co.uk

These organisations will help you gain control of your debt. They will talk with your lenders and help you set up a payment plan to get out of debt. There is no shame in using these groups. They work with thousands of people who face the same problems as you. If you feel helpless to deal with a very bad debt problem, don't ignore it or pray it will go away. Instead, take action, and asking for help may be the first step.

Even if you feel you are drowning in debt,

your story can have a happy ending. Start today to get out of debt, using the ideas I've shared in the last few pages. The lessons you learn in the process will help you enjoy a better life in the future. I know it's true, because I did it myself!

Step 4.
Start to Save

If you are in debt, getting out of debt is an important first step towards financial happiness. To do this, you need to reduce your interest costs and work on repaying the money you owe, a little at a time, until you are debt-free. But those ideas will work only if you make one other essential change: cutting your spending so that debt doesn't grow back. For long-term financial success, you need to change your money habits. Instead of spending more than you earn, you need to spend *less* than you earn. That will allow you to begin saving. Saving, as you'll see, is the secret to a secure and happy future.

Easy, Painless Ways to Cut Your Spending

Look again at your budget worksheet. Are your total expenses greater than your income? If so, that is the source of your debt problem. If you spend more money each month than you earn, the difference must come from debt. And over time, even a small increase in your debt each month will add up, until it becomes a mountain of debt that could bury you alive.

To prevent this, study the spending columns of your budget worksheet. Find places where you can cut the amount you spend. With time and thought, you'll be surprised at how many painless ways there are to reduce your spending. Here are a few ideas to get you started.

- Do you buy lunch, coffee, and snacks at work each day? Maybe you can bring food from home instead. It's much cheaper and it may be more healthy, too.

- Do you spend money every day on travelling to work by bus, train, or car? Maybe you can walk to work (if you live nearby), or ride a bike.

- How much do you spend on entertainment – things like the cinema, shows, sports, parties, and evenings at the pub with friends? This kind of spending has a way of growing over time. Maybe now is your chance to cut back. Instead of going out three times a week, make it just once.

- Do you have any bad habits that you've been meaning to cut out? Work on those habits now, with saving money as an extra reason to change. Maybe you can give up smoking, have fewer pints each week at the pub, or eat one less takeaway a week. If you have a gambling habit, try getting some help. The amount you save from these changes can be huge.

- Do you often buy gifts for your children? Some parents think they must bring home a present for their little ones every month or week. Maybe it's a way of 'buying' their children's love, or of making up for the things the parents lacked when *they* were children. But giving gifts too often is a big waste of money. (Think of all the toys that end up stacked on a shelf in the back of the cupboard.) Instead of spending money on your children, spend time with them; they will enjoy it more.

- Set yourself a daily spending limit. Decide on an amount you can afford to spend each day. Maybe it will be £10 – maybe a little more, maybe a little less. Then carry that amount and no more, in cash, and leave your credit or debit cards at home. In time, you'll find the urge to spend getting less as your habits adjust to the new limit.

- Avoid impulse buying. Before you go out shopping, sit down and make a list of the things you will buy. Then stick to the list. If you spot something else you think you might want, don't buy it right away. Instead, put it on your list for the *next* shopping trip. You may find that, after a week has passed, you don't really need or want the extra item.

- Go food shopping *after* lunch rather than before. Studies show that people who shop on an empty stomach end up buying more stuff than they need, and often throw half of it away. A full tummy makes it easier to resist the tasty-looking treats and luscious smells the food companies use to try to attract your extra pounds.

- Shop for bargains. Whenever you can, hold off on buying bigger things you need, like clothes or homewares, until you spot a sale. Most items go on sale every year at the same time. If you're not sure when the next sale will be, ask a sales assistant in the store. They will usually be happy to tell you.

- Look for ways to save on your fixed monthly expenses. Even basic bills that you must pay every month can offer you chances to save. Spend an evening looking at what you spend on things like insurance, telephone, Internet service, gas and electricity, banking, and other basics. There are many websites with advice on these expenses, as well as bargains being offered. You may find it's easy to save £10, £15, or £20 a month, or even more, just by switching one or two accounts.

- Every month, replace one 'paid-for' treat with a 'do-it-yourself' treat. Pick one thing you enjoy spending money on and replace it with something else that is just as much fun but that costs little or nothing. A day at a football match or bowling? Spend a day in the park or at a local museum instead. Instead of going to the cinema and buying a drink and a box of popcorn, watch a movie at home and make your own snacks. Instead of going to a nice restaurant with your friends, invite them over for a pasta-and-salad dinner.

- And if nothing else works, take the final step: *cut up your credit cards* and close the accounts. That's what I did to stop myself from spending.

Yes, it hurt! But in the end, it made me a stronger, better person. And today, years later, I can carry credit cards and use them wisely because I know that I am in control.

Each of these tips for cutting your spending may save you just a few pounds. But if you try all of them, and come up with some tips of your own, you'll find yourself happily surprised with the amount of extra cash in your current account or pocket. You'll be able to deposit money into a savings account at the end of the month.

Simple Steps to Building Your Savings

Now that you've cut your spending and got any debt problems under control, you're ready for the next big step toward financial happiness. That's starting to build savings.

When you are ready to save, there is a huge tool that can help you. It's called *compound interest*. Here's how it works. When you put savings into a bank account, your money earns interest. (It's like the interest you pay on money you borrow, only it works in reverse. In this case, the bank pays *you*, not the other way around.) For every month your money remains in the bank, a little extra is added, as if by magic. What's more, you don't only earn interest on the money you save. You also earn interest on the interest! (That's what *compound interest* refers to.) The result is that your money grows much faster than you might expect.

For example, suppose you are able to save £100 every month. If you put that money in a jar in your kitchen cupboard or bury it in a hole in your garden, it may remain there safely, but it won't earn any interest. After one year, you'll have £1200. After five years, you'll have £6000. After ten years, you'll have £12,000. And after thirty years, you'll have £36,000.

Not bad. But now look at what happens when your money earns interest. Suppose you put £100 a month into a bank account that pays 4 per cent interest, compounded monthly. (That means the bank pays you interest on the interest once each month.) After one year, you'll have £1222. After five years, you'll have £6623. After ten years, you'll have £14,694. And after thirty years, you'll have £68,912.

That's an extra £32,912 (68,912 minus 36,000) with *no* effort on your part! It's like a gift from the bank just for having an account with them. No wonder people speak about the magic of compound interest.

At this point I should say that since the

economic crisis, interest rates have been very low. This is good news for people in some types of debt but it is bad news for savers, who are not earning as much interest as they have in the past. But even when rates are low, it is still worth saving. Compound interest means that you will build more money – the amount you deposit plus the interest you earn. It is also true that interest rates will not remain very low forever. Now is a great time to get out of debt and get the saving habit.

I hope the example has made you excited about what compound interest can do. It's one of the keys to long-term financial happiness. Over time, compound interest can help you to live in a lovely house, own your own business, send your kids to good schools, take great holidays, and enjoy a happy retirement. But it will work for you only if you start saving, and the sooner the better.

Many people find it hard to save, even when they have worked hard to cut their spending and to get any debt under control. Somehow, by the end of the week, the money in their pocket just seems to vanish rather than ending up safely in the bank. So here are some of my favourite tips for making saving easy. Thousands of people have used these ideas to get themselves started on the road to saving. You can too!

- **Set a savings goal**. Don't just promise to save 'as much as I can' or 'anything extra'. Decide on a real amount per month, per week, or per day. Then treat that as a real promise, not a 'maybe' to be dropped on a whim. If a real emergency forces you to skip saving for a week or two, save more in later weeks to make it up. (And a sudden desire to take a holiday in the Maldives does not count as an emergency!)

- **Save the first pounds from your wages every week**. Most people make a big mistake when it comes to saving. They pay their bills, buy food, go shopping, spend money on daily life and then save the money that is left in their pocket or purse when the week is over. This is backwards! Instead, put savings *first*. As soon as you get your wages, take out the amount you plan on saving and put it right in the bank. Then live on whatever is left. Believe me, you won't notice any change, except when you look at your bank account and watch the amount of your savings grow.

- **Set up an automatic transfer into your savings account**, which is even better than saving the first pounds from your wages. This is a service most banks are happy to provide. Just fill out a simple form and the bank will take the amount of money you choose and put it straight into your savings account whenever you get paid. This way, you won't be tempted to skip savings 'just this once', and the money will never sit in your pocket or purse, crying out 'Spend me! Spend me!'

- **Save the change in your pocket or wallet every day.** Most people come home from work or their daily chores with a handful of spare coins. Get into the habit of dumping all those coins into a jar. At the end of the month, count the coins. If they add up to less than £20, add some extra money and put £20 into your savings account. If the coins add up to more than £20, you're already ahead for next month.

- **Save £1 each working day of the month** – this is another easy way to save £20. Most people have twenty working days each month. So if you drop £1 into a jar each day when you return home, by the end of the month you'll have saved £20 that you can put into your bank account.

- **Tie your spending to saving**. Here's one way to do this. Each time you buy a truly unnecessary or impulsive treat for yourself, your partner or your child, put exactly the same amount into your savings account. So, for example, if you spend £2 on a sticky after-lunch snack at work, put £2 into savings. If you buy yourself a glossy magazine that costs £5, put £5 into savings.

  By the end of the month, you may be surprised to find how much extra you've saved. And years from now, you'll surely get more happiness and pleasure from the money saved than you got from the treats you bought at the same time.

- **Set aside gifts for saving**. This idea, too, can work in several ways. If you get a gift of money for a birthday or holiday, put it into your savings account rather than spending it. If you get an end-of-year bonus from your company, save it. And if your children get gifts of money from their grandparents or other relatives, make a rule that they will save at least a part of the money, perhaps half, in their own savings account.

- **Dedicate your next pay rise to savings**. This is another painless way to improve your savings habit. After all, you're used to living on your current salary. Next time you get a pay rise, start putting the difference into your savings account. You'll never miss the money, since you never had it to begin with. In a year's time, you'll have several hundred or several thousand extra pounds in the bank and those pounds will also be earning interest, making them grow even more.

- **Reward yourself for saving**. We all need a little fun in our lives. So to make your savings programme fun, build in a plan for rewards that you will give yourself when you reach each savings goal.

    For example, if you save as planned for a month, you might let yourself spend £20 on an item of clothing. After saving for three months, you might spend £50 on a day at the beach. After six months, you might splurge with £100 on a really special outfit. And after a year, you might spend £300 on a weekend getaway. But be careful! Don't go wild and spend more than planned, or dip into savings just to increase your fun. And don't reward yourself unless you really save as planned. If you start giving yourself treats 'because I *tried* really hard', or 'because I *almost* made my savings goal', your savings plan will soon fall apart.

Where to Put Your Savings

When you begin your savings programme, ask at your bank about opening a savings account. It's important to keep your savings in a separate account from the current account you use for writing cheques and paying bills.

Even better is a special kind of account called a *limited access* bank account. With this kind of account, you're allowed to take out money only a few times a year. Many people find it helpful to have an account like this that makes it hard to dip into savings except at times of real need. Ask your bank about a limited access account. They'll be happy to help you open one. Then pretend that this account doesn't exist. Don't get a cash card for this account. If the bank sends you one, cut it up. And when making your spending plans, don't think about the money you are saving. Then you won't be tempted to spend it. Ignore this account, except when you check once in a while to see how nicely your savings are growing.

You may also want to think about how to save

in a way that means you won't have to pay tax on the interest you earn on your savings. Here are some ideas for making this happen.

With most savings accounts, you'll have to pay tax on the interest you earn. These taxes slow down the growth of your savings. However, you can help your money grow faster by using two special ways of saving that are tax-free: Individual Savings Accounts (known as ISAs) and National Savings & Investments.

There are two types of ISAs: 1) a cash ISA and 2) a stocks-and-shares ISA. A cash ISA is a special kind of instant-access savings account where you do not have to pay any tax on the interest you earn. In short, all interest earned is tax free. You can currently deposit up to £5100 into a cash ISA each tax year. (A tax year runs from 6 April of one year to 5 April of the next.)

Cash ISAs are very safe. There's little risk that you will lose the money you've made. The only risk is that the bank or building society you have your ISA with goes out of business, in which case, the first £50,000 of your savings is protected. High street banks tend to offer much lower interest rates on accounts you open in the branch. If you are happy handling your savings account online or over the telephone, you might get a higher interest rate.

A stocks-and-shares ISA is for investing. When you deposit money into this type of account, you must select, from a list given to you by the ISA provider, which unit trust or other stock-market product you want your money invested in. The maximum amount you can deposit into a stocks-and-shares ISA is £10,200 each tax year (minus anything you've saved into a cash ISA). All money earned on your investments is totally tax free.

It's important to keep in mind that you are *investing* (this is different from *saving*) money that you pay into a stocks-and-shares ISA. The value of your money will change as the prices of the shares move up or down. You may make a profit if share prices go up, but you may also lose some money if share prices drop. There is no such thing as a risk-free investment. You must always think about how you would feel if you lost some of your money. And if someone tries to sell you an investment saying that it will definitely make you money, say 'no' and keep your money in your bank account. Unless you know what you're doing, you may need some advice when it comes to stocks-and-shares ISAs.

To open an ISA, you need to find an ISA provider who is authorised by the Financial Services Authority (FSA). ISA providers include banks, building societies, investment firms, stockbroking firms and insurance companies. An ISA provider will explain how the different kinds of ISA work so you can decide which is best for you. The whole process is very simple: once you've chosen your ISA, just fill out the proper forms and deposit money into the account. You will need to provide proof of identity and address.

You many also want to use one of the Nation Savings & Investments products as a way of growing your money tax free. These tax-free methods of saving include Savings Certificates and Premium Bonds. They are all available at the Post Office and you can open an account and deposit your money on line, by phone, by post, or in person at a branch of the Post Office. There are also leaflets at the Post Office that explain the products and how they work.

Getting into the savings habit can be a real challenge. But if you try the tips in this chapter, you'll find it much easier. And once the magic of compound interest begins to work, it'll be really fun to watch your savings grow. Best of all, your sense of power, control, and inner strength will grow along with it.

Step 5.
Make Money Work in a Relationship

Dealing with money problems is tough for anyone. Getting to know your own money style and learning how to improve your money habits can be hard. And learning how to control your debts and begin to save is a real challenge, even for someone with a strong desire to do the right thing.

But for most of us, there's one more thing that makes financial success even harder to achieve. It's the fact that most of our choices must be made with someone else – a husband, wife, or partner with whom we share a home, a family, and all the many problems of life. When managing money is a task for two instead of one, the rules become even more tricky.

If you are married or involved in a long-term partnership, I'm sure you've learned how hard it can be to meet the needs of both people fairly. If you are planning to get married or to live with your partner, now is a good time to begin thinking about money matters and how you will manage them together.

Don't make the mistake of thinking that, as long as you love one another, finances will 'take care of themselves'. It's true that love is a big help when problems arise. But money problems can hurt a partnership even when both people are deeply and truly in love.

And don't think that marriage promises a happy, fairy-tale ending. From what I've seen, any money troubles that a couple has *before* the wedding usually become worse afterwards. That's why experts say that more marriages are spoiled by money problems than by difficulties with sex, children, in-laws, or other kinds of trouble. (This fact actually applies to both married couples and couples who are not married. Throughout these pages I will be talking about both kinds of partnership, even when I use the word 'marriage'.)

A couple that is planning to share their lives should spend as much time thinking and talking about money matters as about where they will live, how many children they will have, and what kind of work they will do. And after the partnership has begun, they need to work hard at sharing their feelings, ideas, dreams, fears, and wishes about money.

In the next few pages, I'll offer some thoughts about the best ways to make sure your love partnership is also a happy *money* partnership.

Before the Marriage

Over the years, I've got to know hundreds of couples with money problems. I've found that, in most marriages, money problems are not really about earning, spending, or saving. Instead, they relate to the deeper meanings that money has for people. When people fight about money, they are really fighting about feelings, about respect, sharing, support, honesty, and love. The power of money is that it is caught up in all these feelings and many more.

So when you are getting serious about having a lifelong love partnership with someone, it's a good idea to talk about your feelings about money. Here are some ways to get started.

- Ask about your partner's dreams for the future. For example, what is your partner's idea of a perfect job? How much money would he or she like to earn? Where would he or she like to live? Does he or she have an idea about the perfect retirement? Questions like these can lead to a good talk about where you both want to go in life, and how you will make the money to pay for the journey.

- Ask your partner how he or she feels about saving, debt, and the future. Does he or she have much debt? If so, how did it happen, and what is he or she doing to reduce the debt burden? Does your partner save money each month? If not, why not? What plans does your partner have for building a secure future?

- Share with your partner some of your strongest feelings about money. What is your greatest money fear? What is your deepest money hope? What do you worry about? What do you dream about? If someone gave you a huge sum of money, what would you do with it? If you became poor one day, how would you handle it? Ask your partner to share his or her feelings about the same topics.

- Talk with your partner about how your family handled money when you were growing up. What money style did your parents have? Were they Big Spenders, Cheapskates, Ostriches, Cynics, or did they have a balanced style? How did their money style affect you? Did you grow up to have the same style, or did you turn out differently?

- Share the stories of any money troubles you've had or are having. Notice how your partner responds. When you talk about money problems, does your partner seem thoughtful, helpful, and understanding? Or do they become angry or nervous, or perhaps try to make a joke of it all?

- Talk with your partner about how you handle money – what you do well and what you do badly. Ask your partner to share the same truths about himself or herself. Do you have the same money styles, or are you very different? When you become a team, will you be able to help and correct each other? Or will your failings mirror each other and perhaps make problems worse?

Of course, when you are involved with someone, you learn about their dealings with money through more than just talk. You also get a chance to see how they manage money in daily life.

Does your partner insist on handling all money matters themselves; for example, by paying for every meal, night out, or holiday you share? Do they leave all money matters to you? Or are you able to share money tasks in a way that feels fair to both?

81

Does your partner often seem to waste money? Or does he or she pinch pennies? Does your partner make bad choices when it comes to spending or saving money? Or does he or she handle money wisely?

If you notice something about the way your partner deals with money that makes you worry, pay attention. It may be a sign of deeper trouble to come. Think about your concern, and look for a chance to discuss it. Maybe it is a small problem you can quickly solve, or maybe it means that the two of you have values and ideas about money that are a bad fit for life. These conversations may feel difficult but they can help you to build a much happier future.

Planning the Wedding

For many young couples, planning the wedding is the first chance to manage a big project together. It can be very exciting and fun, but it can also be stressful and scary. If you are making plans for a wedding, think hard about the process, and make sure you work closely with your partner to make it a happy event for all.

Most young people, especially women I think, have a 'perfect wedding' in their minds. It's a dream come true with the world's most stylish wedding dress, gorgeous music, lavish food, and a glorious setting, perhaps on a sunny island or in a hidden, secret garden filled with flowers. Yet few young couples can afford to spend the kind of money that the 'perfect wedding' would cost. Here is the first challenge when planning your wedding. *Decide on a budget that fits your level of income, and stick to it.* After all, the true purpose of a wedding is simply to bring friends and family together to share your special day in a joyous, loving fashion. And that can be done by spending millions of pounds (if you are a rock star or a member of the royal family) or by spending very little.

I've met many young couples who forget this simple truth. Instead, they go a little crazy, chasing their dream of the 'perfect wedding' with no concern about the costs. A year later, they find themselves deep in debt, struggling to pay the rent, and angry at each other. Fading pictures in an album are the only reminder of the day they paid so dearly for.

Here are some tips to keep the costs of your wedding day from being a source of long-term unhappiness and pain for both of you.

- **Make hard choices**. Decide which parts of the wedding are most important to you, and make plans that reflect those choices. Is the music the feature you care most about? Then spend a little less on flowers. Is the food the main thing? Then have fewer fancy cars on the drive to the party, or maybe none at all.

- **Be creative**. Some choices that are simple and less costly can be even nicer than others that are fancy, flashy, and over-priced. Lovely weddings have been held in grand ballrooms, hotels and resorts, and also in backyard gardens, public parks, and beaches.

- **Look for money-saving ideas**. Millions of weddings take place each year, some lavish, some simple. Don't be shy about 'stealing' good ideas from magazines, online sites, friends, and other sources.

- **Join forces with your partner** and promise *not* to spend money just to impress other people. If you find yourself thinking, 'What will our friends and neighbours think?' you are going down a dangerous path. The only thing that really matters is what *you* think.

- **Keep the guest list under control**. It's your wedding, not a party for your parents, family, and friends. You don't have to invite everyone you've ever met. And when people start saying, 'If you invite A, you *must* invite B, C, and D,' beware! That approach leads to a guest list that never stops growing.

- **Avoid thinking that the amount of money you spend is a sign of your love**. Your love for one another is priceless. That doesn't mean the party favours at your wedding must be, too!

- **Try to help everyone feel involved**. If one partner's family is paying for most of the wedding, try hard not to make the other family feel left out.

They say that love is blind. Maybe so. But I hope you'll plan your wedding with your eyes wide open! Believe me, you'll get more happiness from starting your lives together debt-free, with memories of a simple yet joyous wedding, than from a fancy, over-priced event that leaves you saddled with bills it will take years to pay.

During the Marriage

After a glass or two of wine, I like to ask my married friends about how they handle money

85

matters. (Hey, it's my job!) I often think back to what a friend said to me over dinner several years ago. 'My wife and I don't have exactly the same ideas about money. But deep inside, our feelings about money fit each other very well. Most important, over the years, we've worked out when we need to talk about money and when we don't. So sometimes, we work together to solve money problems. Other times, I tackle the problems on my own, or leave them to my wife. In the end, we always find a way to make it work.'

For this couple, the system works well. Over the years I've known them, they've been able to reach many of their goals, such as a second home in the country and winter skiing holidays. And their conflicts about money have been few and far between.

How do they do it? Every month or two, they talk about money. They look at their current earning, spending, and saving, and they talk about what is going well and not so well. They discuss what each wants to do in the next year or two, and talk about what they must do to reach those goals. When their goals conflict, they keep talking until they come up with a plan that makes both of them fairly happy.

My friend Dr Emily Stein is a psychotherapist

in New York. She has helped many couples deal with money problems. Emily says that money troubles in marriage often arise from the fact that money means power. 'It's always bad,' she says, 'when one person in a marriage feels powerless. So if one partner has more money than the other, choices must be made so that neither one feels helpless.'

Sometimes, Emily says, problems can be solved by dividing the family money into three parts: *your money, my money,* and *our money.* As long as the division is clear and fair, this system can work well. In other cases, money tasks can be shared in a way that makes both partners feel important and involved. For instance, if Partner A earns more money, Partner B can take on some extra tasks, such as paying the monthly bills and keeping an eye on the bank balance.

But the same plan won't work for every couple. The key is to sort out a plan that you're both happy with, and then to work hard at keeping the money talk between you open and honest.

Perhaps you wonder which partner in a marriage should be in charge of money matters. In some families, it's felt that the husband should be in charge. After all, men used to be the main bread-winners and money-earners, so isn't it fair that they should make most of the money choices? In other families, wives take control of the money. After all, they often take care of the shopping and make more decisions about the home, so why shouldn't they control the purse-strings? Which of these systems is the best?

My answer is that *both* partners need to be in charge of money matters. The job of handling money and making choices for your shared financial future must be 'owned' by both partners. It's foolish for anyone to say or feel, 'Oh, I never have to think about money. Susan handles all that,' or 'I don't have time to worry about money, so Reggie takes care of it for both of us.' Money is too important to be left to one partner. It affects you both. Both of you rely on it, so both of you should take part in handling it.

This doesn't mean that both partners must share every money task. As you talk about money in the months leading up to your marriage, try to learn about the strengths and weaknesses you each have. Discuss what you both enjoy doing with money, and use these conversations to help you decide who should do what. The big questions are: Who does each task best? Who enjoys the task? Who has the time and energy needed for the task? And is the work-sharing fair?

In most partnerships, the money tasks to be handled include:

- Paying routine bills, like mortgage or rent, electric, gas, telephone or credit cards

- Shopping for food and other everyday items

- Keeping track of your bank accounts and reconciling them as needed

- Handling spending money, which may include giving an 'allowance' to the other partner

- Shopping for special things, like major gifts, furniture, and appliances

- Saving for short-term goals (holidays, for example) and long-term goals (like a house)

- Making choices about saving and investing

- Keeping track of investment accounts

- Dealing with banks, insurance companies, and other financial companies

In most partnerships, these chores will be split between the partners. In some cases, a chore will be shared, perhaps with one partner taking the lead. For example, in the case of big purchases, like a new cooker or TV, you might agree that Sally will research ideas and decide which one to buy, but that she will discuss her decision with Tom before going to the shop.

How you divide the money tasks is up to you. And from time to time, you may want to change the plan to fit your changing interests, time, and tastes.

There are just two important rules: first, be sure you are both clear as to who will handle a money task and how the other partner should take part. Second, don't ignore any aspect of your money just because your partner deals with it.

You know that all partnerships come to an end, whether through death or divorce. Someday, you may have to manage the money tasks your partner is handling today. So at least once a year, go over all the money tasks together. That way, both partners will have a good idea about where the money comes from and where it goes. And each will be ready to handle any problem that might arise.

The Price of Divorce

Today, I really can't talk about marriage without also talking about divorce. Experts say that in the UK two marriages in every five will end in divorce. Naturally, the end of a marriage always means sadness and heartbreak. But it also has heavy financial costs for both parties.

To begin with, getting a divorce is very costly. And divorced couples are almost always worse off than when they were married. They have to pay the costs for two households instead of one, and if there are children, they may have to pay travel costs as the kids go back and forth between homes. In terms of money, there are no winners in divorce.

Of course, not every troubled marriage can be saved. Sometimes divorce is the best choice for two people who are deeply unhappy and unable to solve their problems. So here are my best ideas as to how you can reduce the financial damage that divorce will cause in your life.

- **Look before you leap**. Think long and hard before you make choices about marriage. Make certain that you and your partner have shared feelings about money before you marry. This will help you reduce the chance that financial troubles will lead to a break-up.

- **While you're married, stay informed about your family finances**, keep debt under control, and save as much as you can. This way, if a divorce happens, you will be able to take care of yourself and your children, if you have any.

- **Make divorce a last resort**. Because divorce is so expensive (as well as painful), don't be quick to break up a marriage that may have a chance to succeed. Work at your partnership, be honest with your spouse, and be eager to forgive small flaws. If you can't avoid a divorce, at least you'll know that you gave the marriage your best shot.

If you find that divorce becomes necessary, there are some things you can do to keep the costs under control.

- **Avoid going to war with your partner** over every issue. When you are able to make choices together in a way that both parties feel is fair, without having to use a lawyer to settle disputes, you can save a lot of money.

- **Separate your money dealings** as soon as you know that you will be leaving the marriage. If you have joint bank accounts, divide the money between you and start individual accounts. If you have shared debts, divide those as fairly as you can and put each loan in a single person's name.

- **Buy forms and paperwork online**. If the two of you are able to work together, you may be able to reduce the cost of the divorce by using forms and paperwork bought from a website rather than hiring a lawyer. (However, you should still expect to spend several hundred pounds or more on court fees.) And if your income falls below a certain amount, you may be able to get help with lawyers' bills from Legal Aid, a service of the government.

Love is wonderful. But it's no excuse for acting in ways that are childish or unwise. Think hard about the financial impact of the choices you make, and be sure to give enough time and effort to the money side of your partnership.

Step 6.
Become a Money
Magic Family

The High Cost of Family Life

Having a long-term love partnership makes money problems a bit more tricky. Add a child or two, and things get even more complicated. As you may have heard, raising a child costs a lot. One recent newspaper report about the high price of family living gave the following figures:

Pregnancy and birth	£6,000
Day care	£30,000
Food and clothes	£43,000
Holidays, leisure activities, and birthdays	£21,000
University	£25,000
TOTAL	£125,000

The total is shocking, but the facts aren't quite as bad as all that. As you know, the cost of child-rearing doesn't have to be paid all at once but rather in small amounts over eighteen or more years. What's more, the bills start out small. During the first year of life, the cost of nappies, juice and cereal, and a few items of furniture, needn't amount to very much. By age twelve, however, the usual clothes, shoes, toys, and activities can be quite costly. Hopefully your career and your income will grow as your child does.

Enjoying Family Life on a Budget

But in the meantime, what can you do to keep the costs of family life under control? Thanks to television, kids today are well aware of all the good things that money can buy. If your children are normal, they will soon be bringing you their lists of the toys, treats, and outings they want you to pay for, each more costly than the last. And they won't be shy about using pester-power or guilt as a way to get what they want!

As a parent, you need to keep your kids' money cravings under control. It's important for you because if your family life becomes just a series of fights over things your kids want you to buy, you'll soon run short on patience, money, and brain cells. And it's important for your kids, too. Children who are raised to think that money can buy happiness are doomed to trouble when they become adults and learn that life isn't quite so simple.

There's nothing wrong with spending a little money on treats or outings. The key is to make wise choices about how, when, and why. The 'special treat' that happens every week soon becomes routine. And the child who never learns to amuse himself or herself *without* spending money quickly finds life itself a big bore.

Happily, having a good time on a holiday or during family outings doesn't mean you need to be able to spend without limits. In fact, it's easy to have a great family time while keeping your costs under control. All it takes is planning, setting sensible limits, and being a little creative.

Here are some of my best ideas about how to make the most of family life without breaking the bank. Try one or more of these the next time your kids are asking you to help them have some fun.

- **Use the public library** for a regular outing to find and read books. It's a great place for children to explore the joys of reading, and it costs you nothing. When they find the right book, children can amuse themselves for hours. It also gives you time to catch up on your reading, in peace and quiet for a change!

- **Take your children to the zoo** or on nature walks to look at trees, flowers, or birds. Before you go, use the Internet to find names and pictures of some of the items you may spot. Then make your outing a game, giving a small prize or treat to the child who finds and names the most items.

- **Visit museums and historic sites** with your children. For added fun, make sure you have a goal for the visit. When I take my friend's children to a museum, we go to a special exhibition that I read about before our visit. Then I tell the children some of the strange or funny facts I've learned, making the trip one that the kids are sure to enjoy.

- **Look for local outings that are free or low-cost** at weekends and during holidays. You can find these by looking in the local papers, talking to your neighbours, or checking out the council's website for your town. Many towns offer concerts, films, and other events that are fun and easy to get to.

- **Look for lower off-season prices** when planning a holiday or a weekend trip. Go to 'summer' places in the autumn or spring, for example, or winter ski resorts in the summer. In many cases, the resorts are just as lovely and fun during the off-season, while the costs are much lower.

- **Try to make your travel plans early**, especially if you're taking a break at a peak time, like school holidays or Christmas. You may be able to get good prices on accommodation and airfares. The cost will not be as low as the off-peak fares, but they will be cheaper than waiting until you're closer to the deadline.

- **When looking for a family hotel, search for older places**. Many have large rooms that can be shared by a couple and two or three children. It's a great way to reduce the cost of a family holiday. Also look at new hotels offering special deals.

- **Share your holiday with another family**, or two. If your children get along well with your friends' kids, try going on a holiday together. By sharing the costs of renting a flat or a villa, you will reduce your total costs. But be careful to make some rules about who will cook, clean, and keep the place tidy, so the holiday isn't spoiled by fighting.

- **Ask your children to eat from the Kids' Menu** when you travel. Most restaurants and hotels offer much lower prices on the Kids' Menu, even when the amount of food is fairly large.

- **Don't use the mini-bar** for drinks or snacks. Those items cost a lot. Instead, visit the local food store and stock up on all of the juices, soft drinks, snacks, and other items your children will want.

- **On outings, take your own picnic**. At many sporting events, beaches, and theme parks, food and snacks are costly. If you take your own, you can save money and eat food that is more healthy, too.

- **Look for a credit card that offers rewards** that fit your family's lifestyle. For instance, some offer air miles, others free hotel stays, package holidays, or shopping discounts. This way, you make your money work twice for you, first when you use the card to buy something you need, and second when you enjoy the free reward you've earned.

Try some or all of these tips, and I promise you can have just as much fun as the next family, without taking on the burden of needless debt that spoils the fun for so many.

Raising Money-Smart Kids

Bringing good money skills to family life isn't just about keeping debts low and saving regularly. It's also about raising your kids with the same wise financial values you've learned. Yet many parents find it hard to teach their kids about money. In fact, next to sex, money may be the topic that is most rarely discussed around family dinner tables.

There are many reasons why parents avoid talking about money with their children. One reason is a desire to preserve their children's 'innocence'. 'They'll have plenty of time to worry about money when they're grown up,' I hear many people say. 'Why burden them now?'

Another reason is the belief that children will learn about money in school, in a maths class, for instance.

A third reason is simple fear. Many parents

feel bad about their own money skills, and some are afraid their kids will ask them questions about money that they can't answer.

None of these reasons is a good excuse for failing to talk with your kids about money. Let's start with the idea of childhood 'innocence' about money. The truth is that kids are very aware of money. They hear news about money on TV. They see the amount of time you spend earning, spending, and saving money. They hear the worry in your voice when you talk about the monthly bills, the retirement account, or the savings fund. Chances are good that your children already think about money, and perhaps worry about it. Teaching them the financial facts of life will simply give them tools to master those worries.

Will your kids learn about money in school? A few money skills *may* be taught in a maths class: how to balance a chequebook, how to understand interest rates, and so on. But the real problems with handling money, how to make it, save it, and use it wisely, are not taught in school. In fact, children can only learn them at home, by watching the ways their parents handle those tasks.

Finally, don't worry about your own lack of financial knowledge. You certainly know more about money than your six- to ten-year-old. And there are plenty of good self-help books, including this one, that explain money topics in simple terms. If your child asks a question (for example, 'What's the difference between credit and debit?'), you can simply say, 'I'm not sure. Let's look it up and learn together.'

So there's really no good reason for you, as a parent, to refuse to talk about money with your kids. And in fact, sharing what you know, feel, think, and believe about money is an important part of raising your children. Your kids need guidance from you to learn about the best ways to handle money and the not-so-good ways, too. No one else will do that job. It's up to you.

What's more, raising kids with smart ideas about money will make your family life go better, too. Fights about money have spoiled many a family dinner, weekend, and holiday. Plenty of kids have no idea why their parents handle money the way they do, why they say 'Yes' sometimes and 'No' other times. As a result, they may end up whining when they want something you are not prepared to give them. The best way to avoid such problems is to talk about money, to share your thoughts about it and to answer your kids' questions as best you can.

Once you decide to start on this important

task, here are a few ideas that can help you do a better job of teaching your children about money.

- **Give your child an allowance**. You can begin to give your child a small amount of money every week at the age of four or five, as soon as he or she is old enough to spend it. Having a regular income, even if it's just a pound or two, is a great way for your child to begin to learn about spending, saving, and making choices. Make it a fixed sum. Then review the amount once a year or so, slowly raising it over time as the child's needs change and grow.

  Resist pleas for extra money or endless advances against next week's allowance. A good lesson for small children to learn is the need to plan ahead and use money wisely rather than spending it all at once, as soon as it's received.

- **Take your child to open a savings account**. Between ages ten and twelve is a good time for you or your children's grandparents, or another relative to take them to a bank to open their first savings account. Start the account off with a birthday cheque or another gift. If you like, you can add to the amount with a few extra pounds from your pocket. This should be an exciting moment for your child, a small step on the road to being a grown-up.

- **Make your child save for special purchases**. When they want a big gift like an ipod, a computer, or a video game, tell them to save from their allowance to help pay for it. If the item is costly, and you agree that it is worth having, you might decide to help them pay for it. For example, you could offer to pay half after your child saves half. Don't advance the money to the child, but make them save it, week by week. By watching the savings grow until the great day when the item can be bought, your child will learn about being patient, a useful life lesson.

- **Don't use money as a substitute for love**. Some parents buy gifts for their kids to show how much they love them. This happens a lot during times of family stress or trouble; for example, a divorce, or a time when Dad or Mum has to work long hours and is rarely home. Using gifts as signs of love teaches a bad lesson. Children who are raised this way often grow up to have poor money habits. For example, they may waste money on junk they don't need because they are seeking the love they still feel is missing in their lives.

- **Talk with your child about money**. Share some of the facts about money and life, as far as your child is able to understand them. Are you working overtime to save money to buy your first house? Explain that to your child. It will help them learn to connect extra effort with great rewards. Do you have to cut back on spending because your partner has lost a job? Discuss this with your child. Knowing the cause of the problem will help them to manage their worry better. (It will also keep your child from thinking that *they* are the cause of the problem, something that many children think for no good reason.)

Money ranks with sex and God as one of the most touchy subjects you can share with your children. It's also one of the most important. Don't neglect it out of shame or fear. The more freely you talk with your children about money, the better they will be at handling it as adults.

Step 7.
Chase Your Money Dreams

Most people have a big dream that they think about a lot. It may be to own a lovely home, to have a business of their own, to take a trip around the world, or simply to enjoy a secure and happy retirement.

Dreams like these can be expensive. But if you are able to control your spending, stay out of debt, and save a little money every month, there's no reason why you can't achieve your dream.

The first step is to decide on which dream, or dreams, you want to pursue. They may include both short-term goals and long-term goals.

Short-term goals are those that you can reach by saving for six to sixty months. Short-term goals might include buying a car (new or used), fixing up your home, taking a holiday, or buying new appliances.

Long-term goals are those that you will need to save towards for five years or longer. Typical long-term goals include buying a home, starting or buying a business, and saving and investing for retirement. Nowadays some people also want to save in order to support their children at university or a first job.

Start by deciding which goal or goals you want to reach for. You may want to pick one short-term goal and one long-term goal. If you're married or in a serious relationship, talk things over with your partner. You need to choose goals that both of you are excited about.

Once you've picked the dreams you want to chase, try to figure out how much they will cost. If you are dreaming about buying a new car, visit a couple of dealers to get a sense of the price you will need to pay. If your dream is a cruise in the South Pacific, get some brochures from cruise companies and figure out how much the trip will cost.

If your big dream is retirement, you may need help from a banker or financial advisor. Many people start with the idea that, after retirement, they will need about 70 or 80 per cent of their current income to live comfortably. That's not a bad rule to follow. The hard part is figuring out how large a nest egg you need to save to produce that kind of income. It will depend on interest rates and other factors that can be tricky to guess. That's why seeking the advice of a financial expert can be helpful.

Once you've chosen your one or two biggest

dreams and attached a price tag to each one, the fun begins. Now you simply have to follow these not-so-secret steps to make your dreams come true:

- **Choose the age at which you want to reach your goal**. Of course, the age you choose must be realistic. It takes time to earn and save enough money to achieve a big goal. But it's important to set an age limit. This gives you a clear target to work towards.

- **Put time to work in your favour**. As soon as you can, get out of debt and begin saving. The more you save, the faster your money will grow. Over time, even small amounts of money, added to a savings account weekly or monthly, can grow into a large nest egg.

- **Work out the amount you need to save** each month in order to reach your goal on time. This is easy to do. Many websites have savings calculators that let you work out how different amounts of savings will grow over time at different interest rates. These let you enter a monthly, quarterly, or annual savings amount and then tell you how long it will take you to achieve your goal at that rate.

Then, if you *increase* the amount you save every time your salary grows, you'll shorten the time needed to achieve your goal.

- **Get on the property ladder**. For most people, buying property (that is, a house or flat) is a form of forced savings. Property almost always grows in value over the long term. This means that, when you buy property using a mortgage loan, every mortgage payment you make is a form of saving. This is why most people who are financially secure own one property or more.

- **Change your lifestyle to fit your savings plan**. For most people, this is the hardest part of achieving a big dream. There are two reasons. First, people tend to focus on their income, thinking it shows how successful they are. As a result, when their income goes up, they feel more successful, and this makes them spend more. That's a mistake. If they really want to reach their dreams, they should be saving more instead. Second, people start to think about what they might own or how they might live if they spent the money they are saving. And the more they think about this, the stronger grows the

109

desire to spend. Avoid these dangers. Focus on your long-term goal, and spend less so you can save more.

Perhaps the road to achieving your dream is not as easy as you might like. You may even decide it's more trouble than it's worth. That's fine. Maybe you need to choose a different dream, one that is easier to reach.

But working out what it would take for you to reach your biggest dream is important, even if you decide not to pursue that goal. You may decide that some other amount is your own magic number. It's a very personal choice. One person might decide he needs £75,000 in the bank to feel happy and secure in retirement. For another, £20,000 might be enough. And for still another, just having £500 to handle a sudden problem, a broken-down car, an expected illness, might be all it takes to feel really good about life.

Any of these can be a worthwhile goal. The bottom line is that if you know your own financial dream and truly want to achieve it, there's nothing in the world that can stop you! Why not start today?

Word List

APR (annual percentage rate): The amount of interest charged by a lender for borrowing money. The higher the APR, the larger the price you will pay for the money you've borrowed.

Balance: The total amount you have in the bank or owe on a loan.

Bond: A kind of investment in which you lend money to a company or government. In return, the company or government pays you interest at regular intervals and eventually repays the borrowed money.

Compound interest: Interest paid on interest. When a bank account pays you compound interest on your savings, your savings grow faster.

Consolidation loan: A loan used to repay other loans. Sometimes a person who owes money to several companies will get a consolidation loan in order to repay several lenders, leaving just one (larger) repayment to be made each month.

Credit card: A card that gives the holder the power to make purchases using borrowed money, which must be repaid with interest over time.

Debit card: A card that gives the holder the power to make purchases using money already deposited into a bank account.

Direct debit: When a bank automatically moves money from your account in order to pay a debt or deposit it into a savings account.

Home equity loan: Money that is borrowed by someone who owns a home, using the value of the home to guarantee the loan. If you fail to repay a home equity loan, you may lose your home.

Interest: An amount of money paid for the use of money that is borrowed or deposited in a savings account. When you deposit money in a bank, for example, you are paid interest on that money; when you borrow money from a bank, you must pay interest to the bank as well as repaying the amount you borrowed.

ISA (individual savings account): A special kind of saving and investment account in which your money grows tax-free.

Joint account: A bank or other account owned by two or more people.

Limited access account: A special savings

account that lets you take money out only a few times each year.

Minimum payment: The smallest amount you must pay every month on a credit card or other debt.

Mortgage: A loan used to buy a home. If you fail to repay a mortgage loan, you may lose your home.

National Savings and Investments: One of several kinds of savings account offered by the government in which your money grows tax-free.

Options: A tricky way to invest by betting on the future price of a share or other investment. For most people, options are a good way to lose money, not to make it!

Share (or Stock): A kind of investment in which you own a portion of a company and can receive some of the company's profits in return.

Term: The length of time a borrower has in which to repay a loan.

Quick Reads

Books in the Quick Reads series

Quick Reads

Short, sharp shots of entertainment

As fast and furious as an action film. As thrilling as a theme park ride. Quick Reads are short sharp shots of entertainment – brilliantly written books by bestselling authors and celebrities. Whether you're an avid reader who wants a quick fix or haven't picked up a book since school, sit back, relax and let Quick Reads inspire you.

We would like to thank all our partners in the Quick Reads project for their help and support:

Arts Council England
The Department for Business, Innovation and Skills
NIACE
unionlearn
National Book Tokens
The Reading Agency
National Literacy Trust
Welsh Books Council
Basic Skills Cymru, Welsh Assembly Government
The Big Plus Scotland
DELNI
NALA

Quick Reads would also like to thank the Department for Business, Innovation and Skills; Arts Council England and World Book Day for their sponsorship and NIACE for their outreach work.

Quick Reads is a World Book Day initiative.
www.quickreads.org.uk   www.worldbookday.com

Other resources

Free courses are available for anyone who wants to
develop their skills. You can attend the courses in your
local area. If you'd like to find out more, phone
0800 66 0800.

A list of books for new readers can be found on
www.firstchoicebooks.org.uk or at your local library.

Publishers Barrington Stoke (www.barringtonstoke.co.uk)
and New Island (www.newisland.ie) also provide books
for new readers.

The BBC runs an adult basic skills campaign.
See www.bbc.co.uk/raw.

www.quickreads.org.uk   www.worldbookday.com